Qualms of an Unapologetic

Ritika Jatana

BookLeaf Publishing

India | USA | UK

Presentation by *BookLeaf Publishing*

Web: www.bookleafpub.com

E-mail: info@bookleafpub.com

ISBN: 9789363316560

First edition 2025

*To my forever constant—my Grandmother,
Late Mrs Sheela Jatana;
my mentor and friend for life,
Late Sister Dorothea Perreira,
all my English Teachers, my alma mater
St. Patrick's Junior College (Agra), and
everyone who gave me crucial life lessons.*

*Furthermore, this book is dedicated to all those
who have inspired, encouraged, and challenged
me to embrace the power of words, the beauty
of self-expression, and the courage to navigate
life with grace and resilience. From the halls of
academia to the corridors of life, your guidance
and wisdom have shaped me into the person
and poet I am today. With heartfelt gratitude
and unwavering appreciation, I offer this
collection as a tribute to the profound impact
you have had on my journey.*

ACKNOWLEDGEMENT

- Rhymezone.com for my love of rhyme and rhythm
- Thesaurus.com and Merriam-Webster Dictionary for synonyms, antonyms, and meaningful verbiage
- My previously written Haikus, Couplets, Sonnets, Quotes, and more that inspired me during frozen thoughts
- Chat GPT Open AI for inspiration during creative blocks
- A few illustrations Designed by Freepik

PREFACE

In the pages that follow, you will embark on a journey through the labyrinth of my thoughts, emotions, and experiences. Each poem in this collection is a reflection of my innermost self—a testament to the highs and lows, the triumphs and tribulations, of a life lived with passion, purpose, and imperfection.

"Qualms of an Unapologetic" is more than just a title; it's a deeper peek into the real thoughts and emotions we often overlook in the busyness of life. It's an ode to the hustler, the overthinker, the giver, and the dreamer within us all. Through the rhythm of words and the melody of verse, I invite you to join me on this journey of self-discovery, introspection, and transformation.

As you immerse yourself in these pages, may you find solace in solitude, courage in vulnerability, and strength in the unbreakable spirit of the human heart. For in the progression of life, it's our flaws, our fears, and our vulnerabilities that make us truly authentic—and undeniably human, unapologetically!

INDEX

Unapologetic for the Soul I Bear!...... 1

A Pocket Full of Roses......3

The Wrong Way......6

Free......7

Eyes...... 8

The Art of Solitude (Part 1)......10

The Art of Solitude (Part 2)......12

The Call...... 14

The Girl Who Overthinks......16

A Perfect Day...... 19

Mean What You Say......21

The Field......22

We are Confused!...... 23

Ghosts of Choices......24

Chaos...... 25

Just a Lazy Day...... 26

Two-faced Men......28

The Wardrobe Saga...... 30

Angels and Demons......33

Let the Tangles be!...... 36

Who's the Fool?......38

All Sizes Matter!......39

Be Kind!...... 41

Survive......42

The Real Battle.................................43

Stay Strange.................................44

Dear Love!.................................45

It's Okay!.................................48

Consideration.................................49

Baby Squirrel.................................50

Change.................................52

Barter of Breaths.................................53

Forged in Fire................................. 55

Hypocrisy................................. 56

Let it be!................................. 57

Windward................................. 58

Hustle Hard.................................60

The Vibes.................................62

Consistency.................................64

The Universe................................. 66

My Hair................................. 68

Broken Angel.................................70

Unapologetic for the Soul I Bear!

I seldom stand in the mirror gaze,
Truly flawed in more than many ways…
A thing of beauty, though rare is there,
Unapologetic for the soul I bear!

My body tells a story from every phase,
From the happier times and the hurtful days…
Remembering the cries for what I'd now least care,
Unapologetic for the soul I bear!

Adorning the curves that turn the heads,
Some in awe, some in mock, others to jerk in their beds…
The sneers, the taunts, Oh! the sharp tear,
Unapologetic for the soul I bear!

"You must fit in, trim your edges, be neat!", they
say,
A bold cry dying to shriek, but low I lay…
Horrid or defying, in their eyes, I stare,
Unapologetic for the soul I bear!

I am not the mold they get to carve, the shape
they desire,
It takes a fight, day and night, but I keep the
fire…
I roar back harder at the growls, yes, I dare,
Unapologetic for the soul I bear!

For real is hard, authentic takes the road uphill,
Fighting norms is no new, you see, I know the
drill…
Letting whispers fade, and judgments stay clear,
Unapologetic for the soul I bear!

Fraying my scars, crowning my flaws,
I cry, I laugh, up my guard, and file my claws…
No wealth to ward, no heir to declare,
Unapologetic for the soul I bear!

I'll dance my rhythm, sing my melody,
For it's my life, not their parody…
Yes, I'll fall and hurt, yet rise and repair,
Unapologetic for the soul I bear!

A Pocket Full of Roses

Just like a chicken from a hatched egg,
Just as a bibber craving for his last peg...

I saw her—a running nose I remember,
And to cover her, there was no fur...

She stood at the florist's corner, she wanted
those flowers,
At her home if at all, surely there were no jars...

I also recall some bruises on her feet,
In a long time, she had nothing to eat...

Roses, lilies, carnations, and orchids,
Never meant anything until trapped in her
eyelids...

Suddenly I felt sweat in the chill—all perplexed,
My scarf, jacket, and stockings were turning me
vexed...

A patched vest and a ripped-wrapped cloth,
At home last night, I had fussed over a simple
broth...

It felt like a river between the two ever-apart
banks,
Never had she seen learning, and we are still
combatting ranks...

We go to movies and silver, gold, or platinum
seats we choose,
Alas, that right in life but we lose...

It was neither sympathy nor a shock,
On a closed door of a lost thought, it was just a
knock...

She personified unseen, unheard, unsaid
torments,
It didn't feel she needed walls to dwell, but
certainly the vents...

Her charm had struck me that I wanted to
preserve,
I have way too much, not even sure if all of that
I deserve...

I wanted it sooner—before my momentary ardor
closes,
I felt myself alive in her, she smiled back at
me—when I stuffed her with a pocket full of
roses...

The Wrong Way

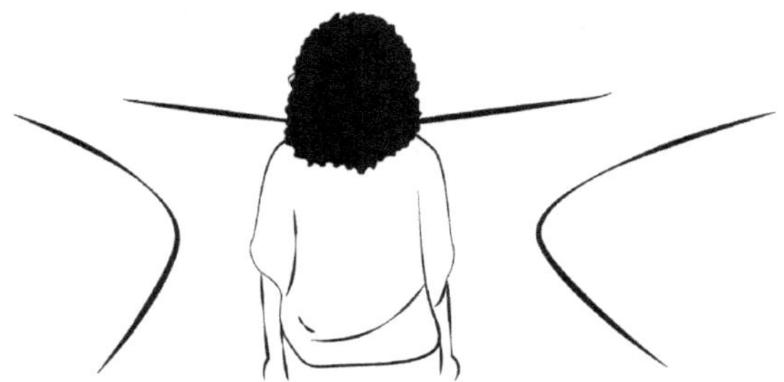

They said I took the wrong turn,
That I'd get lost, that I'd crash and burn.
But here I am, still on my feet,
Turns out the wrong was not the defeat.

Some detours are long but sweet,
Filled with adventure and new snacks to eat.
The "wrong way" had some splendid views,
Makes me think it's time to accept my muse.

Who knows the path, not planned—
is exactly where I'd make my stand.
For sometimes the "wrong way" may be a bit
long,
But after all, you'll reach where you belong.

Free

For once, I want to be free.
Free from the noise, the endless plea.
Free from the ache, the constant fight.
For once, I want to sleep—please, let me sleep
tight.

Eyes

They show you the world;
And the world, the world within you...

You may murmur all the lies,
They'll shout only what's true...

They capture what you like,
And store it all nice...

They alarm you about the bad,
Even when you aren't that wise...

They are the angels who are—
smaller in the bright and bigger in the dark...

They sleep with you, cry with you,
Show off your fire with their spark...

They're gorgeous, they're tireless,
They're precious, no matter the size...

You may sham all that laughter,
But what goes inside, is all in those EYES...

The Art of Solitude (Part 1)

Where darkness is beautiful and so is day,
Where December is dainty and so is May...

Where I delve into myself a little more,
Where I tend the wounds that have gone sore...

Where I meet not agonies but also bliss,
Where I explore depths I often miss...

Where I shed off the skin of despair,
Where there's resonance and a lot of self-care...

Where there are quiet corners that do not haunt,
Where there's desolation but also its want...

Where there's rest and also wander,
Where there are lessons and mistakes to
ponder...

Where the journey is the haven—and no rush,
Where there's no disguise, no hush...

Where there's no one to hide from, no one to
intrude,
Where you're your most real self, nothing to
delude...

It's neither a phase that's crude, nor a bad mood,
It is the land of awakening, the art of
SOLITUDE.

The Art of Solitude (Part 2)

For solace is a blessing and not a fight,
It is like meditation and not a poor plight...

So seek solitude with a humble heart,
For it is pure, true, and not a world apart...

In its immense depths, humility may rise,
Not where arrogance musters in withdrawal's
disguise...

The echo of narcissism is possible in quiet and
serene,
There's a thin line between being distant and
mean...

For it's easy to fall prey on isolation's verge,
Remember, it's when you're alone, that your true
selves emerge...

Solitude isn't a summit so seek no reward,
In the vastness of its alms, it's a double-edged
sword...

For it may consume you altogether or give you a
fresh start,
So, find the balance, my friend, for SOLITUDE
is an art!

The Call

Hark! Do you hear?
That sound's now near...

What first seemed cheer,
Is now noise causing the wear...

It's all turning grey from Rhodo,
There are more to fall like the Dodo...

It is all falling apart,
In need of a false double-tap heart?

When there's a need to turn to minimals,
We are turning into vogue hoarding criminals...

Mind it! If it's all not dealt,
All of this beauty continues to melt...

For it's your choice to be the seraph or the
cockatrice,
To bring back our Earth, or to run towards the
apocalypse!

The Girl Who Overthinks

In the depths of her thoughts,
In the labyrinth of her soul,
A girl tiptoes lost,
So no water drops from her bowl...

A prisoner of doubts,
Shackled in the shadows,
Caught in the storm,
While escaping tornadoes...

Between the masks she wears,
And her true face,
She's trapped and tired,
Running a solitary race...

Unseen and alone,
Wandering to find her home;

Amidst expectations and true desires,
She continues to roam...

Gulping the silence,
And drilling the chaos,
Baffled whether to rejoice the applause,
Or remorse identity-loss?

Seized in norms,
Eluding the moments gone,
She sews the fragments of others' lives,
With her own spirit torn...

Afraid to hurt,
And strong to fight,
Falling somewhere in between—
the wrong and the right...

Longing to be loved,
Craving to feel whole,
Giving everything in her might,
Not knowing her role...

She does love herself,
Yet gazes approval,
To listen to the world,
Or continue with her heart's perusal?

Pacing to find love,
She's too blind to see,
The greatest love lies within,
Shouting to be free...

There's no destination.
It's the journey's story to be told,
To enjoy loving herself,
And to break the mold...

For in embracing her truth,
She'll continue her way,
And the love she seeks,
Will forever stay!

A Perfect Day

A sky of blue where fluffy clouds play,
Serene greens, merry chirps—on a bright sunny
day.

My kitty and I—we roam out and about,
He's afraid of noise, but he's allowed to shout.

A pretty open cafe down a cute street,
My purr-mate and I take the best seat.

I order our favorites and start to play,
And since it's a perfect day, he doesn't run away.

Quite a poser, he catches a lot of eyes,
I touch up my makeup, in case someone tries.

He gets his treats and I get mine,
Happy upbeat music, some cheese, and wine.

Happy to the soul, contented to the brim,
We laze around and hear the waves as the lights
go dim.

Good hair, nice pictures, and no calories turned
to fat,
My cat and I return to our flat.

He continues to rule, I endlessly cuddle,
It's all squeaky clean, absolutely no muddle.

While it's my ballad of a perfect day full of
delight,
(Whether or not any of this happens) With my
cat by my side, everything's just right!

Mean What You Say

Speak with honor, let actions display,
Mean what you say, no covers to sway...

The blade of candor cutting through the fray,
Promises kept, come what may...

Where darkness dawns, be someone's ray,
With words of substance, integrity will pay...

For there's no more just black and white, there's
also grey,
Cut to the chase, be direct, no wordplay...

And when it's time and you call it a day,
"He meant what he said", the word will stay!

The Field

It's toxic, this need to miss,
To open doors that lead to an abyss.
Smelling the air that opens the scar,
The tunes that play gloom from afar.

Fearing visiting those lanes,
Washing the blood of dreams down the drains.
A promise for afterlife to change the plight,
A place beyond the worldly wrong and right.

"In that field, we'll meet someday," it was said,
And then it all ended, it badly bled.
And maybe there's no field, no world beyond,
There's no need to meet, there's no such bond.

This world's better, and it's better to be away.
Nothing more to live, nothing more to say.
Even if it hurts once more—goodbye!
It's all silence there—no smiles, no cry!

We are Confused!

We hold what we want to throw!
We pluck what we want to grow!
We cling when it's time to drift!
We linger when it's time to swift!
We starve when we should eat!
We turn faces when we should greet!
We dream, we pray, we run after it all day!
We are reminded in ways but we drive it away!
We keep craving it until it's time to get!
We get—and all the toil we forget!
We let it go after all the fuss!
We run behind what's right within us!
We gotta open our eyes before it's too late!
We keep seeking happiness that's right at our
gate!

Ghosts of Choices

Every choice leaves a shadow behind,
A ghost that haunts the corners of the mind.
Hushing, "what if," and "could have been,"
Flickering in the dark with an irking grin.

The roads not taken, the turns skipped—
Maybe, those were better—I should have
tripped.
They fade but never disappear,
The ghost of choices—always near.

Haunting or guiding, hard to tell,
A glimpse of heaven or a taste of hell.
We still look for them, and they always show—
They are the ghosts—the only ones we know!

Chaos

Chaos hums a familiar tune...
Pain and peace dancing in the same room.
Risking it all, diving in headfirst…
Sometimes it's the mess that's the thirst.

The storm inside, a place to roam,
In the chaos—I find my home.

Just a Lazy Day

In the realm of hustle,
sometimes my laziness reigns...
And I tell this to myself,
please! No need for strains!

A day of laughing,
and no more race...
Just kick back and chill,
in my favorite place!

I'll be back hustling tomorrow,
but I will laze today...
In all of this rush after all,
I deserve a day!

Let the earth rotate,
and I take my time...
Let them fight the wars,
while I sip my fresh lime!

So, grab a pillow,
a cozy cocoon...
Laziness, my friend, sometimes
is a delightful boon!

Two-faced Men

In a world full of two-faced men,
deception sneaks in every den.

Smiles that are bright and word as sweets,
they spin their webs with sly greets.

One face for the world and another covert,
a mask of charm you could barely avert.

Behind the closed doors with lies and plots,
grace on the facade, on the rare evil trots.

Their fabricated facts with subtle guise,
no matter the strong wit, you'll be lured to think
twice.

Beware their smiles, skip their advice,
for in their baloney, the trap lies.

Be ready, for you can't escape the charade,
up your game, wear the mask, and join the grand
masquerade.

And if you don't, you'll remorse the betray,
so gulp it now or learn the hard way.

Use your head until diplomacy aced,
guard up, and join the two-faced!

The Wardrobe Saga

An evening of reverie, I was lost in trance,
I started fathoming what I most glance.

My mini world, where all my secrets lie,
I started talking to my wardrobe while passing
by.

She started whispering softly, with a little sigh,
"Dear owner, a bit of restraint, a little stop, why
don't you try?

For you are drowning in the retail sphinx,
Please have some mercy, release me of this tuffy
jinx!"

But, Oh!, the thrill of the retail satiety,
Is like a calming balm for my anxiety.

With every swipe and each click,
I feel my worries start to flick.

From dullness and death, I become alive,
As one by one, those packages arrive.

Of course! I know I go overboard,
But, hey! I work for it, I can afford.

What now? You talk all self-love and now you judge?
I know the closet's bursting but I won't budge.

I have it all and I still yearn,
More shoes, more bags, and dresses to earn.

I do like minimal—sleek and neat!
But, oh! Those urges, I can't defeat!

Don't get me wrong, I try to pare it down,
Alas! A woman's impulse is a legit renown.

Amidst this chaos, I find my peace,
In lovely soft fabrics and jewels that please!

So, though my wardrobe may protest and it pleads,
I decide to keep indulging in my retail needs.

As to you my wardrobe, I make the vow,
I'll rein my greed but not right now.

For in those racks and shelves of delight,
I find my joy, my eyes shine bright.

And as I continue to clean and organize anew,
I promise my wardrobe, I'll always be true to
you!!!

Angels and Demons

Light without darkness is just a dream,
And nights, sometimes never-ending they seem.

Within the depths of the soul, the whirls unfold,
Where demons hide, their stories untold.

Yet in the murk, angels find their voice,
For it's through shadows they make their choice.

The demons within, the beasts—they roam,
They're a part of me, I am their home.

To concede them is to hold the key,
To balance the forces, both wild and free.

For demons won't die, they have to dwell,
You know it's right here—the heaven and the
hell.

Let the devils sleep where they're meant to hide,
In the corners of the core, let them abide.

And let the angels rise and awaken my soul,
Let the light spread and grace take control.

I cling to my angels, and keep burning the flame
within,
To let them guide me through the thick and thin.

I still won't shun the demons' cry,
For they are too, a part of the sky.

So I let them speak, let them be heard,
But in their grasp, I don't get deterred.

For both are crucial in the grand scheme of life,
In the balance of chaos, of peace, joy, and strife.

Darkness after all is the absence of light,
And bad is black—the dearth of good and white.

As I keep learning to tame my devils with all my
power,
I let my angels dance as my soul buds into a
flower.

I love them both equally, and do you know why?
Because they are both within me and not up in
the sky!

Let the Tangles be!

In life's intricate web, we find,
tangles that perplex the mind.
We strive to unravel each knot,
knowing not everything's for us to sort.

Acceptance is a soothing balm,
not all struggles are ours to calm.
For in the conundrum of fate's design,
some mazes are not mine.

Letting be is not defeat,
trust in what the universe will meet.
For seeds we sow and dreams we chase,
find their rhythm in time and space.

Releasing control is not to shirk,
it's becoming a part of the greater work.
And in the melody of the cosmic hum,
our roles and paths will gently come.

Some currents are beyond command—
don't need struggle but for us to withstand.
So, let's be the light in shadows deep,
while the Earth has its secrets to keep.

The choice to hold on or to let wander,
for a butterfly, is prettier when flies yonder.
Finding the balance is the ultimate fun,
for good isn't good if we expect in return.

And with kindness as our big power,
we continue to navigate near and far.
Affirming dreams yet believing in flow,
some things to keep, and the rest—letting go!

Who's the Fool?

Am I a fool, easy to play?
Believing it all that they say?

Am I shy or just making my move?
Why to say—nothing to prove?!

All Sizes Matter!

They say, "All sizes matter," but only if they are
right—
Not too loud, not too quiet—also be polite.
A little too loud, a little too proud,
And suddenly, among the norms, you aren't
allowed.

You are told to speak but only when it's neat,
Cannot be that bold nor too offbeat.
But speak too soft or a tad unsure,
You now need to be, a little more mature.

Every opinion has its place,
But only if it "rightly fits the space."
Step out of line, and there's a glare—
Like you've broken a rule—how'd you dare?

They say all voices should be heard,
But language should be theirs, word by word.
A voice that's small, too soft, is quickly ignored;
The louds are suppressed, the ones that once
roared.

It's funny, isn't it? The way they decide—
Who's worthy of the seat and who's pushed
aside?
You can be the loudest, the smartest, the best—
Still, you won't measure, you won't pass the test.

But here's the truth, if you get to see,
We are all here struggling to be free.
Not defined by what we wear, how we say,
But by how we live and love every day.

So maybe one day, when the judgment ends,
We'll realize we are all just imperfect trends.
It's not the size nor any measure that's the key—
It's just being human—being you and me!

Be Kind!

Leave a little kindness wherever you go—
A smile, a word, a hand or so!
Maybe your wish is too far to see,
But through you, someone else's might just be.

You owe nothing, still give with grace,
And watch how the universe works in its ways.
Sprinkle your charm wherever you tread,
No one's watching, but the news will spread.

With your kindness, the load of others gets
lighter,
You'll see how the world shines a little brighter.
The pains are sore, the cuts deep—let's sew,
And see how the universe works its magic
through you!

Survive

To survive and strive, can't always play by the rules…
Pretend not to know—keep fooling the fools…
To live in a lost world—being yourself is the best of tools!

The Real Battle

We bicker and battle—over trivial schemes,
While the world drowns in what we call our
dreams.

The oceans are choking, the air's turning grey,
And we are just busy—fighting a pointless fray.

We hoard and waste—with blind eyes, reckless
hands,
Ignoring the earth, as it slips through the sands.

The real war is creeping silently—just right now,
But we are too busy, too stubborn to bow.

And when it's all gone, what will be left to fight?
The world we have ignored—fading out of sight.

Stay Strange

Alone's not bad—no debates, no mess,
No waiting on texts, no need to impress.

Eat what you want, binge what you like,
No sharing chips—no one to psych.

Everything fades, no one remains fair,
So why not just breathe your own air?

No one to judge, no plans to rearrange,
In a world so dynamic, it's nice to stay strange!

Dear Love!

Oh! Dear Love!
I took you to get me on my knees,
to make my heart numb and my spirit freeze.

Dear Love,
You were supposed to make me go crazy and
mad,
to make me yearn for my beloved and deeply
sad.

Dear Love,
I heard you were a charm that casts a spell,
for you, lovers fight the world and every power
they repel.

Dear Love,
You are known to make people insane,
you cause tragedies and so much pain.

Dear Love,
I should have known you better,
for you certainly cannot be confined in a letter.

All the theories seem shaken,
Heck, I was always mistaken!

Dear Love,
For you are the one that gives wings to fly...
You are the one who wipes tears and stops cry...

You set the spirits free from dungeons into
light...
You fix the broken and give them might...

You deliver wit, strength, and reason to live...
You prosper minds and teach how to selflessly
give...

You show dreams are illusion and the real is
beauty...
You infuse kindness that's not mere duty...

You release statues from jinx and spells...
You bestow courage to come out of shells...

You push to try, achieve, and rise...
You free from the shackles of fictional lies...

You dare to be bold and heal from the past...
You motivate to swim across the ocean of life so
vast...

You lift the vulnerable to feel and breathe...
You calm the rages ready to destroy and seethe...

You soothe, you defend, you heal, you inspire...
You complete, you repair, you make me love
myself and admire...

Dear Love,
I wish I had known you better,
I wish they had known you better...

And because I didn't know you any earlier, I am
the confessor...
We deserve you as is, not speck lesser!

It's Okay!

It's okay to be unsure, to feel small,
Like a leaf trembling of where it will fall.
To stand in the fog, and not see the way,
Wondering if I'll ever find the light of the day.

It's okay to be scared, and to take things slow,
Like a brook unsure of where it should flow.
For it's not always about being brave or bold,
It's also embracing the shivers and when the feet
turn cold.

It's okay to take time and let the qualms unwind,
Not all the answers are at once to find.
Not everything always needs to be figured out,
It's okay not to be okay—without a doubt.

Consideration

The truest love is silent care…
A thought of them even when they aren't there...
It takes its steps to guard your heart…
Holding your peace in every bit and part!

Baby Squirrel

In the garden beneath the Peepal tree,
A baby squirrel learned what life could be!

The sun kissed its fur, the frost bit its toes,
Each day a battle, but that's how it goes.

It watched the birds soaring free and high,
Also, the ants building empires, try after try.

It jumped and climbed the bark with falls and
grace,
Tumbling and jumping all over the place.

The cat came close with hunger in its eyes,
But a twist, an agile leap—the squirrel survives.

Watching strange beings, making friends too
soon,
Laughed in the sun, and wept under the moon.

Dogs, bees, rabbits, and mare,
Some stayed, some left—but the world didn't
care.

A bitten apple, a rotten bread, a nice nut in a
while,
Rains drenched it at times, and often, springs
made it smile.

Through storms and hunger, fighting to strive,
Climbing each branch, learning to thrive.

It chased the rays and embraced the rains,
Found joy in little things, even through pains.

Just a baby squirrel—small and spry.
What a beautiful being, though—oh my my!

But hey, that squirrel's grown, don't you see?
Does it sound like you—or maybe it's me?

Change

Change is never soft nor kind,
It stirs the heart and bends the mind.

A storm of doubts, a leap, a fall,
Yet beauty lingers through it all.

And in its chaos, truths unfold,
New beginnings written—brave and bold.

Barter of Breaths

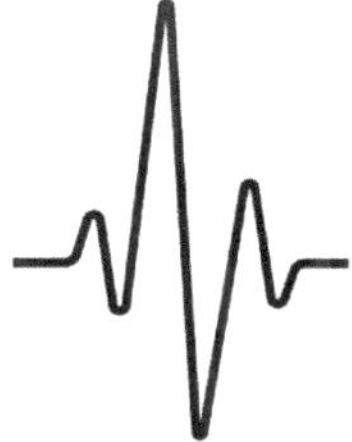

In a world that's far and unseen,
In the yarns of, "would have been...",
I think of a place where there's no fate,
Live as much, breaths for the exchange rate.

For some, it's bitter and cold,
A burden too massive, a pain untold.
Their hurt is never ending, emptiness all across,
They need rest, tired of the albatross.

For some, on the other side, it's unfair and fast,
Counting breaths that they want could last.
Reaching for mercy, hopeful to stay,
To chase the dawn, to live another day.

So what if, in the world afar— that distant land,
There could be the account of breaths in one's
own hands!
No judgments passed, no remorse to bear,
A simple trade of life— the true meaning of
"share"!

Where weary could give, the willing could take,
Prayers all answered, no lives at stake.
Where breaths could be shifted—so much so—
From those who end to those who grow.

The place where no one pleads—
To live or to die—one gets what one needs,
The world where they listen to the unsaid,
Where life is chosen, not always led.

For where we stand in the world we know,
Counting unknown breaths, no balance to show.
No mercy for the agonies and dreams die a
thousand deaths,
That world could be so much better—with
'Barter of Breaths!'

Forged in Fire

Reality or delusion?
Oh pain—what are you?
Fact or illusion?

Slowly towards rest,
Beginning with turmoil so heavy,
A rock on the chest.

A heart that runs—
on a searing hurt—
Not paining as it was once.

Not hardening as stone,
But embracing the wounds,
Calling the storm home.

Forging is an art—
For flames may cut deep,
Yet pain is my part.

Hypocrisy

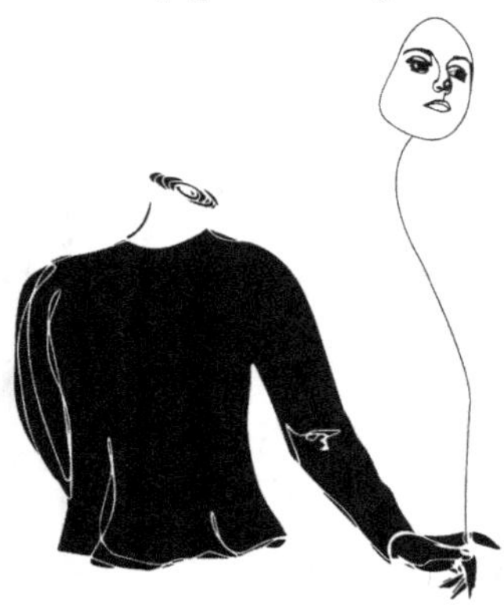

Oh! Hypocrisy, you crafty chameleon,
You sway the world, you barbarian!
With a wink and a nod, they signal and they
play.
One color in the night, another by the day.

Oh! The mighty roars of their righteous
conviction,
The next moment strayed in contradiction.
While promises of gold, stones to find,
Hypocrisy is a spell—one of its kind.

Tangoing with the heart, forcing heads to twist,
Hypocrisy's game is a devilish tryst.
For in its jinx, truth and lie are alike,
A perpetrator for the world as well as one's
psyche.

Let it be!

Tried to fix the chaos and it laughed in my face,
So I shrugged, grabbed my drink—and gave it
some space.

Turns out, when I stopped the frantic spree,
Life sorted itself—who knew? I just had to "let
it be!"

Windward

The hardest truths are the simplest,
You won't ever have to ask for love, care, or
interest.

You focus on effects, thinking you are the cause,
For if you have to run after it, it's not yours—it
never was.

"If I try harder, I give more, they'll notice, they'll
change",
It doesn't work that way, darling, you know it,
it's not something strange.

Clenching the sand too tight only spills it away,
Pulling further from yourself—the more on your
heart it will weigh.

Know that letting go is heavy, but it's not defeat,
It's reclaiming your energy, or you'll dry, you'll
deplete.

Love doesn't grow with force, pleas, and
withhold,
It strengthens you, nurtures you, blooms
effortlessly without being told.

To fit a mold, you don't have to twist,
For if it's real and meant to be, you will rise and
feel your spirits lift.

So, what you give outside, redirect it inward,
You'll see the magic—energies, love, and calm
flowing windward.

Hustle Hard

In the hustle's fire, time bows to will.
Yearn for more, heart shouldn't be still.

For the energy you put out is the energy you get
back.
Forget mastering, know multiple trades, be the
Jack!

And age is a number, a state of mind.
So, learn new stuff, and leave your doubts
behind.

No settling for less, no compromise.
In the pursuit of passion, Phoenix will rise.

So dare to endeavor, don't stifle the spark.
Forge your path and leave your mark.

Do not stop, don't retard.
Go on, go get it, keep hustling hard!

The Vibes

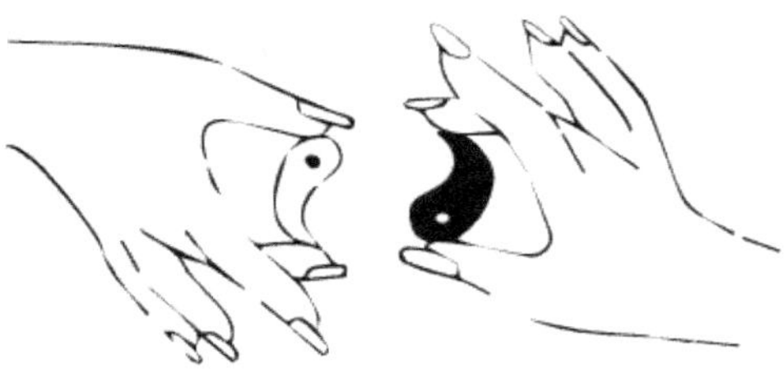

I've always believed the world is a web of vibes,
Every bit emits aura, there's an energy it
imbibes.

While we talk energy, it's both dark and bright,
Negative is a bummer, and positive shines a
dazzling light.

Ever experienced how magnetic is the positive
charm?
Makes everything better—a sudden shift from
chaos to calm.

A strong positive will have the nasty withdraw,
And all pure souls—children, animals—would
naturally draw.

As for strong auras, you could easily tell,
They're liked and trusted—all woes they quell.

Around them the toxics wriggle and frown,
As the dynamos turn their energies upside down.

So, choose your energy wisely, feel who are you around,
Sense the vibes of everything, for they're not just in the sound.

Consistency

In the beginning, everything feels new,
Every word bright, every gesture true.

The effort is easy, the expression grand,
Every moment feels perfectly planned.

But time settles the rush as it always will,
The chatter quiets, the air grows still.

What once felt effortless, now asks for care,
A soft reminder—to all the more be there.

It's not always fireworks, not always fun,
It's showing up even when you want to run.

It's listening—even when tired and spent,
Choosing to stay if that's the intent.

Consistency isn't loud, it's steady and pure.
It's an unsaid promise to always be sure.

To water the roots, especially when dry,
To hold it close, to not let it die.

For it's in the small acts that often fade,
To keep the spark that was there when you
swayed.

As love in any form isn't just a start,
It's keeping it alive, tending each other's heart.

And if you really want it, if you care to stay,
Consistency will turn it into forever someday.

The Universe

The universe is a quiet artist, painting what you
see,
Your mind's whispers holding the key.

Think of sunshine and it lights your way,
Shadows on your mind and they are here to stay.

It's as if the cosmos is hosting this cheeky game,
Always reflecting what you think—both wild
and tame.

Picture a smooth drive, green lights all through,
Dread a jam and it's bumper-to-bumper
hula-baloo.

Focus on the wind and the glory is in sight,
Worry too much and nothing goes right.

You dream of peace and calm fills the air,
Start fearing worse and stress will start to dare.

The universe isn't cruel—nor kind,
It simply mirrors the state of your mind.

So think with care and let your mind align,
You see—the universe, after all, directs your
storyline...

My Hair

In the course of my ardor, my hair have taken
the grind...
Each of my strands—a story of its own kind...

With tangles, waves, and frizz all there...
You have been with me, a crown that I wear...

In rushed days and nights unwound...
My hair, you are always to be found...

You covered my acne and scars alike...
Wiped my tears when melancholies spike...

It hurts me if you wither away...
I hold you tight in my sway...

So judge me on time and money spent...
You, my hair, deserve every cent...

For you have been like next of kin…
You make me secure in my own skin…

Stay with me and I'll always care for you…
And in your shadows, I find my real hue…

Broken Angel

In the depths of her being, a tempest roars,
With endless battles, her spirit soars.

She is a keeper, yet a lot more,
Seeking understanding and finding her cure.

Her scars are a testimony to the fire she has
walked,
Of the tears that have fallen and the tears that are
locked.

Scared of losing and of inflicting pain,
Fiercely loyal through every strain.

She hides her torment and hustles to strive,
She fights hostilities, determined to survive.

She longs for peace, for moments of calm,
To forget expectations and the social qualm.

She hears every voice as her own echoes lone,
Talking to herself, creating her clone.

Hoping to be free, from all the masks she wears,
To run unfiltered, without the worldly cares.

Her walls are high and trust gone thin,
Armoring her soul, shouting from within.

Yet beneath the layers, a flicker of hope,
Her love doesn't die, she knows how to cope.

A woman that falls and fights, fathoms and
flows,
Twirls and smiles through thorns under toes.

So if you choose to walk with her, tread with
care,
For the love that oozes from the broken—is the
most rare.

www.ingramcontent.com/pod-product-compliance
Lightning Source LLC
LaVergne TN
LVHW041226200726
843507LV00013B/2589